DAILY EXCEPT SUNDAY . . . CN mixed train 233 trundles over the Port Rowan Branch at 12 mph in the charge of a 4-6-0 built in 1910. JOHN A. REHOR.

CANADIAN

2829

ROBERT HALE.

STEAM!

EDITED BY DAVID P. MORGAN

CANADIAN PACIFIC

A KALMBACH PUBLICATION

Library of Congress Catalog Card Number:
61-18532

First printing, 1961
Second printing, 1964
Third printing, 1968

For Margaret Joyce, who by believing all
things possible, caused me to believe,
too. And also because she agreed that
the Rhodesia Railways plate was a
serious matter.

Don Wood.

I am neither a prophet, nor the son of a prophet, but I believe that many in this room will live to hear the whistle of the steam engine in the passes of the Rocky Mountains and to make the journey from Halifax to the Pacific in five or six days. — Joseph Howe, 1851.

FOREWORD

1 SO MUCH could be written and yet so little has been published about the Canadian steam locomotive that one scarcely knows where to begin. For one thing, no other nation owes more to steam than does Canada, because when Parliament finally signed a contract with the Canadian Pacific in 1880, a national division, as significant as, if less bloody than, America's recently concluded Civil War, was imminent. A decade before the Dominion had achieved independence on paper, but its lifespan was problematical so long as the 3500 miles between its coasts were bonded by nothing more economic or enduring than the tracks left by trappers' snowshoes and Indians' moccasins. During the flower of the Victorian Era Americans were wont to think of Canada's fledgling sovereignty as an "adventure," and an English opinion weekly declared the land west of Ontario "about as forbidding as any on earth." The Government was caught between jeers that a transcontinental railway would be a "foolish and fantastic waste of money" and the fear that unless rail was spiked westward Manitoba would begin dumping its wheat in the U. S. and British Columbia would secede altogether. It might even be intelligently argued that Canada's valid day of independence was November 7, 1885, for that was when the final spike on Canadian Pacific between Montreal and Vancouver was driven home at Craigellachie in Eagle Pass, B. C. Yes, and when a conductor could call out (as he did), "All aboard for the Pacific!"

So the steam locomotive, by forestalling secession and implementing sovereignty, was a political instrument as well as a civilizing agent. In Britain and on the Continent the railway merely supplemented an organized system of roads, rivers, and canals. In Canada rails bridged the awesome distance between a largely coastal colony and an integrated and independent nation bordered by the Atlantic and the Pacific.

Only the steam locomotive could have conquered Canada. The challenge was more than simply the sheer distance across land masses remote from east-west water channels. It was distance dissected by rivers, mountains, muskegs. And it was distance north of the 49th parallel where zero was mild and the snowdrifts were deep and unyielding. Contractors invaded such distances with armies of men and horses, tons of dynamite, even primitive track-laying machines; and railroaders followed in their wake to hold the line with that all-purpose, all-weather machine: the simple, sturdy, wood-burning diamond-stacked 4-4-0.

This heritage of Canadian railroading had a discernible influence upon locomotive design which is apparent today even in dieselization. Whereas the United States by its economy favored many specialized regional systems, Canada was obliged to orient itself around two true transcontinentals (which between them account for 90 per cent of the Dominion's rail mileage today). And these systems lacked both the traffic density and the economic incentive for the motive power of unusual wheel arrangement, speed, tractive effort, and/or size which a Missabe Road or a Santa Fe could justify. Canadian locomotive design naturally evolved toward a standardized, relatively simple all-purpose machine of modest axle loading. There were few exceptions to the rule — only six articulateds . . . only ten engines in our time with driving wheels as large as 80 inches . . . a season of compounds at the turn of the century but only one genuine experimental since. Rather, the transcons required and bought universal locomotives that could haul sleepers or wheat with equal ease, burn oil in Alberta or coal in Nova Scotia, and exchange parts with sisters working the breadth of a continent away.

But if the objectives of the two transcontinentals in the matter of steam motive power approximated one another's, their rosters did not. History authored the difference to a degree. Uncompromised by either merger or nationalization, Canadian Pacific was standardizing and even constructing many of its locomotives a generation before Canadian National was born of what John W. Barriger has termed "a heterogeneous collection of 22,000 miles of bankrupt railroad" (or to quote present CN President Donald Gordon, "a polyglot inheritance of Government lines built or acquired without hope of profit"). Heterogeneous, too, were the 3265 locomotives that came into the CN fold in 1923 from the roundhouses of the Canadian Government, Canadian Northern, Grand Trunk, Grand Trunk Pacific, and their subsidiaries in the U. S.; and for a season the vast amalgamation showed scant evidence of charting a motive power course of its own. There appeared the oddity of Belpaire-boilered Mikes, a set of orthodox 4-8-2's, and five Santa Fe's which, by virtue of 57-inch drivers, managed to be the most powerful locomotives in the British Empire. In 1928 and 1930 respectively, the system acquired the first two passenger diesel road units in the hemisphere and five 80-inch-drivered Hudsons.

The wheel arrangement destined to become the locomotive trademark of the National emerged from the erecting halls of Canadian Locomotive at Kingston, Ont., in 1927 in the shape of the 6100, a beetle-browed 4-8-4 credited to the design of CN mechanical chief C. E. Brooks. Initially dubbed "Confederation" type (but later Northern in deference to Northern Pacific, which had introduced the 4-8-4 just seven months earlier), the engine was first proudly displayed to the American Railway Association's Mechanical Division convention in Bonaventure Station, Montreal, in June, then dispatched to Baltimore & Ohio's Fair of the Iron Horse, where she really forecast the future of steam far more accurately than did such entries as Pennsy's K4, a Western Maryland Decapod, and a D&H high-pressure compound. The 6100's commanding, nay, ferocious, looks belied her vital statistics. She looked big because of her overhanging Elesco feedwater heater, all-weather cab, booster-fitted trailer truck, and 12-wheel Vanderbilt tank, but the fact of that matter was she possessed an engine weight of just 194 tons and driving axle loadings less than those of a heavy U.S.R.A. 2-8-2. For CN this was ideal, for she could get about in Pacific and Mike territory, taking 18-degree curves in the process and alternating her versatile 73-inch drivers between limiteds and manifests. She could work across two or more divisions without change, too. More than 200 4-8-4's of successively refined detail followed the 6100 onto the rosters of CN and its U. S. subsidiary Grand Trunk Western, and they constituted the prime mechanical agent in the reformation which was and is Canadian National.

The orderly evolution of engines on Canadian Pacific was in the Pacific and Mikado era when CN was formed, but the privately owned transcon declined to place so much confidence in a single wheel arrangement. Indeed, CP spurned any eight-coupled wheel arrangement for dual-service work. A pair of company-built 4-8-2's of 1914 were never duplicated nor were two exceptionally handsome home-made 4-8-4's of 1928. And though the railway believed in the dual-service principle with the same fervor of its nationalized rival, it indulged in a broader choice of types, purchasing 4-4-4's, 4-6-2's, 4-6-4's, 2-8-2's, and 2-10-4's more or less simultaneously until dieseldom. CP countered North American design trends in other ways, too. Instead of always buying progressively bigger power, the system bought in 1944-1948 102 Pacifics whose

engine weight of about 115 tons was only slightly more than that of the road's first 4-6-2 of 1906 and substantially less than its heaviest 162-ton 4-6-2's. All during the 1930's U. S. builders urged their clients to replace obsolete, downgraded secondary mainline and branch-line locomotives with light but modern units specifically designed for such duties, but CP was the only major system on the continent to implement such a policy. Also, CP was the only road to buy Hudsons in large numbers — 65 of them — for dual service. And CP was one of only two roads (Milwaukee, with its ponderous Hiawatha Atlantics, was the other) to obtain four-coupled steam speedsters (Jubilee 4-4-4's 3000-3004) as an alternative to articulated diesel lightweight streamliners in the 1930's. All of these Canadian Pacific locomotives had in common a capability that excelled their comparatively modest dimensions, not to mention as inimitable an appearance as ever stamped a road's roster in our time.

The component inseparable from everyman's image of the Canadian steam locomotive was the Elesco closed-type (i.e., the water passed through a series of tubes surrounded by steam; there was no mixing of the two) feedwater heater. Seemingly, if not quite in fact, every new CN and CP locomotive constructed after 1925 bore an Elesco, either unashamedly hung out over the headlight for all to see or sunk almost out of sight in the upper front end of the smokebox; and literally dozens of older engines were visually modernized by the application of Elescos. Few peoples have any more legitimate cause for heating boiler feedwater or anything else than do the Canadians, but nevertheless one suspects that the Superheater Company's headquarters in New York must have included a gold-framed oil portrait of the salesman who acquitted himself so nobly north of the 49th parallel. It was this bundle-type auxiliary more than any other one external characteristic which lent the Canadian locomotive an air of authority and size quite out of proportion to its statistics. The Elesco made an impact on other roads — C&O, for instance — but never on other nations.

Another factor which endeared CN and CP to train-watchers was the half-century of Dominion locomotive history under steam which both afforded right up until dieselization. Canadian Pacific was the purist's delight, for tucked away for the night in a remote New Brunswick roundhouse one could discover an old Consol with high-pitched headlight that was physically unchanged a whit since she'd left the erecting shop in 1907. Ten-Wheelers fronting mixeds banged past depots on whose walls hung publicity murals of the 4-6-0's double-heading wooden limiteds out of Connaught Tunnel. As for the modern power, one could have almost any choice in a class: with or without streamstyling. Hudsons, for example. The original 2800's of 1929-1930 were handsome, almost rakish creatures with boiler-tube pilots, visible feedwater heaters, obvious domes. But dating from 1937 there appeared what were soon to be officially known as Royal Hudsons (by express permission of the British Government to commemorate Their Majesties' 1939 visit) — identically dimensioned 4-6-4's but semi-streamlined with recessed headlights, contoured pilots and running board skirts, and domeless boilers. Each series doubtless had its supporters, but the point is that CP refrained from modernizing the appearance of the first 2800's to conform with that of the newest. The charming virtue of Canadian National, on the other hand, was that it didn't exist at all until after World War I. CN proper, then, never bought an engine smaller than a Pacific or a Mike. Instead one found in its roundhouses Grand Trunk Moguls, Intercolonial 4-6-2's, Canadian Northern Consolidations — all of the polyglot power, standing in their stalls cylinder to cylinder with each other and the latter-day Northerns. Which was stimulating, at least for the American visitor, because the inherited locomotive was a rarity in the U. S. One *could* locate an ex-BR&P Mallet on the B&O and an SA&AP 2-8-0 on Espee's T&NO, but their presence wasn't axiomatic as it was on CN. As for the system's own designs, the Northerns came in a variety of formats which had outside engine-truck journals, vestibule cabs, and Vanderbilt tanks in common but which differed in sandboxes, smoke deflectors, feedwater heaters or exhaust steam injectors, and driving wheel designs. The original 4-8-2's were blood relatives of the 6100-series 4-8-4's, but the last Mountains of 1944, 6060-6079, resembled nothing else in the hemisphere, much less on CN, for these "Bullet Nosed Bettys" had cone-nosed smokeboxes and full-fledged flanged stacks.

There was never a setting for steam that surpassed Canada. The endless oceans of prairie between the St. Lawrence and the mountains permitted the traveler to board his train, dine, read, and enjoy a full night's slumber — then arise to find the same inexhaustible 4-6-4 holding down the front end. The Canadians dispatched their relatively small rigid-framed engines into Rockies and Selkirks that Americans would not have dared attempt without articulateds, and the brooding peaks echoed back the thunder of triple-headers in contests with gravity of revered memory. And then, of course, there were the elements — the ice and sleet and snow; the thermometers reading 54 degrees below; the line wires hanging low with 2¾ inches of ice on them; the ghastly "blue ice" that had to be hand-chipped

out of switchpoints with picks or burned away with oil; the cold so intense that engines steamed up roundhouses until visibility vanished; the engine water shortages that occurred when supply lakes literally froze to the bottom.

Many might argue that the tranquility of Canadian railroading was its finest recommendation in the not-too-distant days when smoke still rose above the land. Say the two-story red frame depots (the agent lived upstairs) that slept the long Quebec afternoons away under horizontal order boards, awaiting the return of the mixed that had gone up the branch when dew still lay in the meadow. Or the hush that fell upon the huge waiting halls of Winnipeg or Regina once the Continental or Dominion had departed west. Or yet the occasional thump of the air compressor on the running board of a 4-6-0 waiting at the junction for the mainline train from Ottawa.

And finally there were the names: Riviere du Loup, Teeswater, Moncton, North Bay, Medicine Hat, Red Pass Junction, Capreol, Field, Portage la Prairie, Revelstoke — romance names and railroad names. Names on station boards clutched by icicles, names in operating timecards stuck in the pockets of overalls riding a thousand bouncing seatboxes, names called out across the red plush of coaches with floors gritty with cinders. Oh, the names as well as the towns, junctions, and cities they identify are with us yet, but they'll never be quite the same as when they were accessible only by the steamcars.

This book professes to be, with qualification, a pictorial audit of Canadian steam, for to its publisher and editor it has seemed proper that a photo sampling of rods and exhaust and high iron in the Dominion should be given the permanency of hard covers. The volume concerns itself exclusively with the standard-gauge activity of the two transcontinentals (and a subsidiary or two) on grounds that the independents are so numerous and diverse as someday to merit a separate volume unto themselves. Also, the photography has been purposefully selected to qualify for the definition of "in our time" because the intent of the editor is to remind rather than to instruct.

No attempt whatsoever has been made to inject into this book geographical balance or to illustrate all principal engine classes or wheel arrangements. Individual print quality was not necessarily a criterion. Instead, *Canadian Steam!* seeks only to sample pre-diesel railroading as it related to the locomotive and as it was experienced by those who ran and rode and watched the trains of CN and CP. Insofar as the lens permits, we have sought to recall the blast of open pops and the retort of the Alemite gun as a division-hurdling 4-8-4 was serviced near midnight . . . the manner in which the mixed train's passage complemented the pastoral farmlands of Quebec in fall . . . the rise and fall of ten-coupled side rods over Selkirk elevations . . . the screaming blur of a Hudson running well over 90 . . . and the gurgle of condensed steam through the open cylinder cocks of a dying Ten-Wheeler awaiting the boiler inspector.

Canadian Steam! is for the perceptive, for those who having eyes, saw; and having ears, heard. May this book remind them of what we can never forget. **1**

ABOUT THIS BOOK: A member of CN's regional p.r. staff in Montreal, J. Norman Lowe, first suggested the propriety of a hard-cover book devoted to Canadian locomotives; and once Kalmbach Publishing was committed to such a project Mr. Lowe gave unstintingly of his time and knowledge in its marketing. Quick approval of the project came from Publisher A. C. Kalmbach, for Al yields to no man in his affection for the engines of Canadian National and Canadian Pacific — as anyone familiar with his 8500 railroad color slides can verify. Those concerned with the creative work on the book saw in it an opportunity for an American answer to the extraordinarily imaginative railroading publishing now reaching us from the Continent and the Orient. For each print included, at least three were considered; the layout artist, Ted Rose, was given carte blanche to evolve a fresh and uninhibited format, but each photo cropping was examined and many were revised in design conferences with Art Director David A. Strassman and the editor. All three of these had experienced the subject firsthand and possessed deep convictions on its image. Rosemary Entringer is responsible for the freedom from typographical errors as well as the discipline of the editor's grammar. The photographers whose credits appear herein made this book possible, of course, and they are the men responsible for any merit it has. Committing the image of steam to film remains difficult, demanding, infrequently rewarded work, especially so in northern climates, but the following pages indicate that many were equal to the challenge. Finally, the selection of photography, choice of engines, statistical accuracy, and expression of opinion herein are the editor's responsibility and any failings in these areas are his alone.

— D.P.M.

MAIN LINE

CANADA was possessed of the breadth to enable steam to
exploit every ounce of the magic implicit in the words "main
line." Mainline operation connoted relays of 4-8-4's rolling the
green cars of the Continental 2924 miles from the banks of
the St. Lawrence to the shores of the Pacific, and it meant
a pool train Hudson picking her way into Windsor Station
through the smoke laid down by the Pacifics accelerating
commuters out of Montreal. But the "main" also suggested
endless miles of single-track train-order territory on which
the enginemen of 2-8-2's read aloud sheaves of flimsies
before venturing forth from the security of a siding. Troop
trains and wheat extras off the prairie, speed as fast as
75-inch drivers could revolve, the event that was the
Dominion — all this was the "main."

MONARCH ON MANIFEST . . . Royal Hudson 2845 sends a spire of

oil exhaust skyward as she nears Winnipeg with the hotshot Soo Freight under her wing. L. A. STUCKEY.

ROLLING 'EM . . . Bullet-nosed Mountain 6076 races along
near Oakville, Ont., with No. 80. J. P. LAMB JR.

CARRYING WHITE . . . Technically Extra 6217 East,
the third section of the Inter-City Limited, a mile east
of Port Hope, Ont., on the CN. DAVID PLOWDEN.

ARRIVAL . . . Engineer of CN Pacific 5600 eyes waiting express traffic as he brakes into Palmerston, Ont., with an Owen Sound-Toronto passenger train. The 4-6-2 began life on the books of the GT. HERBERT H. HARWOOD JR.

I THINK I CAN'T . . . CN Mike on Extra 3253 East stalls atop grade near Brighton, Ont., because of tonnage. DAVID PLOWDEN.

LOCAL . . . Palmerston-London train
No. 171 — two cars and Pacific 5588 —
pauses before depot at St. Marys, Ont.,
on CN. DON WOOD.

FORE AND AFT . . . Northerns
6181 and 6175 at Moncton, N. B.
PHILIP R. HASTINGS.

CAPACITY: 12,000 GALLONS . . . CP 4-6-2 2380 loads water at the plug in Swift Current, Sask., before coupling onto an extra east to Moose Jaw. ROBERT HALE.

HIGHBALL! . . . Extra 2380 East, en route from Swift Current to Moose Jaw, Sask., knifes the cold of December with steam-generated speed. ROBERT HALE.

WHIR OF WALSCHAERTS . . . Mountain 6029, one of the original locomotives purchased by CN after its confederation, wheels a Montreal local out of Ottawa with a style befitting a high-wheeled Hudson. D. L. McQUEEN.

EXAM . . . A flashlight probes feedwater pump of Hudson 2831 during No. 44's pause in Regina. ROBERT HALE.

CONFERENCE . . . Engineer and conductor of CP No. 44 consult at cabside under gaze of Hudson 2829's fireman. ROBERT HALE.

NATIONAL'S NOTABLES . . . A pair of 4-8-4's fill the night air with

sounds of blowers and turbogenerators and pumps. JIM SHAUGHNESSY.

WATER LEVEL . . . Pacific 2707
hurries CP No. 2 east along the banks
of Burrard Inlet a few miles out of
Vancouver. ANDRE MORIN.

ONTO THE MAIN . . . An
elderly Pacific assists a Mike out of
the siding at Cookshire, Que., with
CP tonnage. JIM SHAUGHNESSY.

THE RARE K . . . No. 3101, one of only two 4-8-4's on CP's roster,
climbs upgrade from Magog, Que., with the overnight St. John-
Montreal Atlantic Limited in tow. JIM SHAUGHNESSY.

PRAIRIE COUNTRY . . . The smoke of CP No. 1200, a light and modern 4-6-2 of postwar build, dusts the consist of No. 55 near Woodman, Man. FRANKLIN A. KING.

STOP, LOOK & LISTEN . . . The Pacific leading CP Extra 2709 West toward Vancouver whistles for a grade crossing at Dewdney, B. C. DAVID W. SALTER.

MAGIC . . . The wonder of faraway places is summed up under the platform lights as a Royal Hudson, blower on and pops hissing, prepares to be off. A. C. KALMBACH.

PACIFICS . . . 4-6-2's of CN and CP create white steam and smoke patterns in Toronto. A. C. KALMBACH.

ONCE MORE, THE PRAIRIE . . . CP passenger bridges the North Saskatchewan River departing Edmonton, Alta., and accelerates south toward the wheatlands and Calgary. CANADIAN PACIFIC.

WINTER

THE most-talked-about operating statistic in Canada in the
winter is the snowplow mileage of the transcons. It is
nonrevenue, expensive, time-consuming, unavoidable mileage,
and in steam it was synonymous with the towering exhausts
of as many as three locomotives behind a single plow.
Winter also dictated the all-weather vestibule cabs of all
the newer steam power and necessitated double-heading
as boilers were taxed to the limit to supply steam heat
as well as traction. Winter could congeal the oil in the
journal boxes of a way freight while its 2-8-0 was dropping
off a single car, and winter could sweep away sand before
it could steady drivers clutching at an icy rail. Winter, indeed,
had but one redeeming virtue: low temperatures and snow
made possible such photography as appears herein.

WHITE STUFF . . . Elderly (1912) CP Consolidation 3722 has her high headlight burning as she mothers a cut of 25 cars across the timbers of the Great Hog Bay trestle outside Port McNicoll, Ont., in heavy snow. A. JORGENSEN.

UNDAUNTED . . . Northern 6170 shrugs off wet, sticky snow as the head-end cars of her

CN train take on express. TOM MILLER.

LONG LOOK . . . Engineer of CN Pacific 5293 examines his charge before leaving Sherbrooke, Que. JIM SHAUGHNESSY.

ILLUSION . . . CP local seemingly skates on frozen lake as it runs down Gatineau Rive

Valley near Cascades, Que., to Montreal. D. L. McQueen.

NE PASSEZPAS . . . CN 5300 clears Sherbrooke, Que., en route from Portland, Me., to
Montreal with train 17. JIM SHAUGHNESSY.

WINTER MEET . . . Mixed M117
holds the main in chilly weather for a
meet on CP with First 82 at Benson, Me.
PHILIP R. HASTINGS.

OVERHEAD . . . Ice-choked St. Lawrence River poses no problem to CP subsidiary Quebec Central's local No. 6, which sweeps over CN's Quebec Bridge. PHILIP R. HASTINGS.

SMOKE AND STEAM . . . CP Pacific 2588 works local upgrade out of Cookshire, Que. JIM SHAUGHNESSY.

ANOTHER GREEN RIVER . . . Crew of CN First 710 deserts warmth of caboose to look over westbound extra headed by Pacific 5258 and Mike 3313 at Green River, N. B. It's shortly after dawn, but snow obliterates sun. PHILIP R. HASTINGS.

NEAR SUNSET . . . On a late January afternoon CP Ten-Wheeler 990 trundles empty reefers through East Lyndon, Me., en route to the potato warehouses of Caribou with local No. 85. H. BENTLEY CROUCH.

COLD . . . Mountain 6000 of CN's eastbound Continental Limited bores through the B.C. Rockies in subzero weather after a heavy snowfall. RAIL PHOTO SERVICE: EARL C. STORM.

FLUFFY EXHAUST . . . CN Mountain 6071
thunders past Bayview Tower en route to
Toronto with Inter-City Limited. JIM SHAUGHNESSY.

AT 95 MPH . . . Royal Hudson 2823 roars down the St. Lawrence Valle

...toward Quebec City with train No. 362 in tow. JIM SHAUGHNESSY.

BRANCH LINE

IN common with the United States, Canada is honey-

combed with rails. The Victorian railway fever spawned

too much duplicate mileage and too many lines into nowhere.

A measure of the Canadian railway problem today is the fact that

too many branches are trying to exist on truckload traffic.

Yet whatever dilemma the mixed train daily in steam created

for the auditors in Montreal, it was a boon to those enchanted

by small engines and short trains. Long after air horns had

drowned steam chimes in the U.S., schedules as infrequent as

once a week were maintained on hundreds of miles of branches by

Moguls and Ten-Wheelers and Consolidations. In New

Brunswick there was even a 44.6-mile branch patrolled daily

into the 1950's by 4-4-0's of 19th century construction. Those

who rode the branches then will long remember.

SYLVAN SCENE . . . Ten-Wheeler 425 pilots CP mixed through the foliage

etween Campbell's Bay and Fort Coulonge, Que. JOHN A. REHOR.

LEANING INTO IT . . . CP 4-6-0 417 lifts sizable tonnage upgrade out of Shawville, Que., toward Waltham with enough momentum to flap her white flags. JOHN A. REHOR.

THIRSTY . . . The section gang stands aside in Campbell's Bay, Que., as D4g Ten-Wheeler 417 on the CP way freight from Ottawa eases up to the plug for a long drink. JOHN A. REHOR.

CONVENTION . . . CP Ten-Wheelers meet in Sharbot Lake, Ont.; the 840 blows off following her arrival with local from Renfrew and 1087 looks on. Don Wood.

L.C.L. . . . CP Ten-Wheeler 970 is all the train-watcher could ask as she sweeps through Milan, Que., with the merchandise car and caboose of the eastbound peddler between Sherbrooke and Megantic. JOHN A. REHOR.

LEGENDARY . . . No one who saw or heard or rode the celebrated May 1, 1960, CP fan excursion triple-headed through Ontario by American 136 and Ten-Wheelers 815 and 1057 will ever forget that cold, climactic day. At dusk the extra is bound for home at Snelgrove. DON WOOD.

MORE OF SAME . . . Triple-header charges upgrade at Forks of Credit. A. JORGENSEN.

REMOTE . . . Freshly cut lumber trails the tank of oil-burning CN 2-8-0 2141 on Holt Creek trestle, B. C., in the seldom explored interior of Vancouver Island. DAVE WILKIE.

SHORT . . . Only two cars separate engine and van as CN 5578 steps down grassy single iron at Clandeboye, Ont., on her way home to London. TED ROSE.

TRANQUIL . . . CN 2-8-0 2141 barely ruffles the quiet of virgin territory as she works empty flats west to the loggers a few miles out of Victoria, B. C. HERBERT H. HARWOOD JR.

EXTRA WEST . . . CP 946's six-coupled drivers drum across a steel bridge at Eastray, Que., on a way freight. Bunker has been built up to boost coal capacity of the 4-6-0. JOHN A. REHOR.

ALL OUT . . . CP mixed 659 climbs away in the rain fro

leads 11 cars off the carferry from Ohio, a combin

he dock at Port Burwell, Ont., along Otter Creek. Ten-Wheeler 1061

d caboose, and receives assistance from 4-6-0 888. JOHN A. REHOR.

TYPICAL . . . Again the essence of the
branch line is spelled out as CP mixed 612
nears Sharbot Lake, Ont., with a ubiquitous
D10e 4-6-0 on the head end. DON WOOD.

FULL OF INTEREST . . . CN 4-6-0 (departing Elmwood, Ont., with the way freight extra north to Owen Sound) is bound to engage the enthusiast with her tall stack and vertical bell hanger, inboard piston valves, shielded whistle, and embossed numbers. JOHN A. REHOR.

SILHOUETTE . . . At dawn a westbound CP peddler etches itself against the horizon while crossing Lac Petite Magog at Deauville, Que., en route to Farnham. JOHN A. REHOR.

THE DAY BEFORE DIESELS . . .
Unkempt CP Consol 3722 trudges toward
Orillia, Ont., with the way freight from
Port McNicoll on April 30, 1960. The
following day diesels took over the system's
last all-steam branch line. DON WOOD.

AGAIN, THE 3722 . . . Some 3000 feet of the Great Hog Bay trestle is traversed by high-headlighted CP 2-8-0 as she departs Port McNicoll, Ont., for the last time on the branch to Orillia. DON WOOD.

CLOSE-UP

TWO comparatively modern and liberal schools exist in railroad photography. One advises backing off from the approaching train so that its habitat is exposed too instead of merely the engine and its consist, the other closing in on the locomotive so that even the rivulets in the hot grease on an axle end stand out like rivers. The shape of the Canadian steam locomotive made it an especially worth-while subject for close-ups, whether the camera was exploring the piping complexities of an Elesco heater or the primeval simplicity of Stephenson gear. Was the crown on a 4-6-4's skirt painted or embossed? Were the outboard journals on a Northern's engine truck solid or roller bearing? Did an old Pacific mount an automatic stoker? The camera, at short range, looked long and told all.

OPEN POPS . . . The safety valves of a CN 4-8-2 lift
in the engine terminal at Saskatoon and hurl a cascade
of steam into a December sky. ROBERT HALE.

POWER . . . From cylinder to crosshead on a semi-streamlined CN 4-8-2. ROBERT HALE.

TRANSMISSION . . . Beneath the skirts of the 6060, a disc-drivered
CN 4-8-2 delivered just prior to dieseldom. ROBERT HALE.

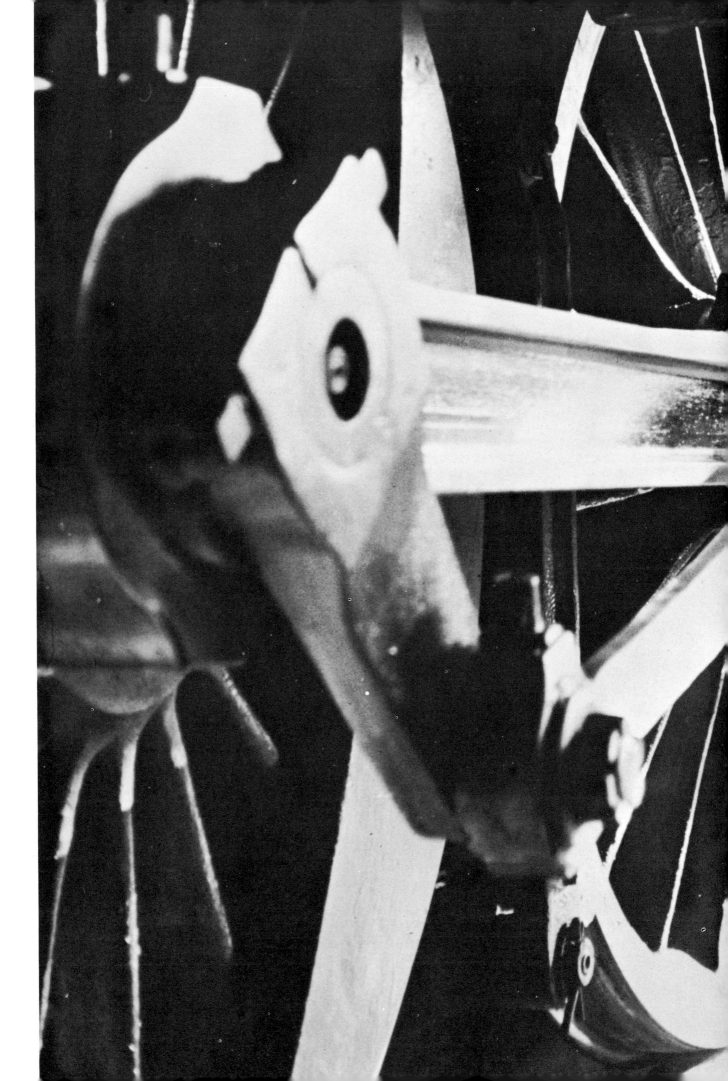

RODS . . . The setting sun filters through roundhouse windows at Three Rivers, Que., and glints on a CP Pacific. JIM SHAUGHNESSY.

HEAD-ON . . . Clearly numbered CN 4-6-2 5123.
ROBERT HALE.

FACES FACE TO FACE . . . Smooth cone
nose of a postwar 4-8-2 contrasts sharply with
exposed plumbing of an earlier breed of engine
on the CN at Saskatoon. ROBERT HALE.

SAD . . . Recessed headlight
accents glumness of a G3g Pacific
displaced by CP diesels and drained
of all life. Bruce R. Meyer.

A CLASSIC . . . CP 2-8-0 3722 by night. A. Jorgensen.

HIGH DRIVERS . . . Royal Hudson and Pacific exchange confidences on CP ready track in the Moose Jaw terminal. ROBERT HALE.

CLEAN . . . Drivers and rods of a CP Royal
Hudson display evidence of steam cleaning
in a terminal close-up. J. NORMAN LOWE.

DISTINCTIVE . . . Cone nose and flange stack of CN 4-8-2 No. 6073. J. Norman Lowe.

BALD . . . Simplicity keynotes CP Hudson. Bruce R. Meyer.

MOUNTAIN

THE original and/or shortest rail crossing of any given mountain range is usually the route which pays for its boldness in helper districts. Therefore, in this book Canadian Pacific is given exclusive possession of the mountain chapter because CP topped the Continental Divide in 1886 via the spectacular Kicking Horse Pass and spiked steel west to even steeper gradients in the Selkirks, whereas the Canadian National traversed the Divide by way of the Yellowhead Pass route of 1914, the easiest crossing of any railway on the continent. CP tried and defaulted on the Dominion's only articulateds in an effort to negotiate its grades, then turned to ten-coupled rigid-framed locomotives which finally evolved into booster-equipped and semi-streamlined 2-10-4's whose exhaust must echo yet.

BIG JOB . . . Smooth-of-snout Selkirk 5921 looms against a backdrop o

836-foot Cascade Mountain near resort of Banff, Alta. CANADIAN PACIFIC.

ENGINEER'S VIEWPOINT . . . A Decapod pilots the Dominion's 2-10-4 through
Kicking Horse Pass. RAIL PHOTO SERVICE.

IMMENSITY . . . Double-headed limited
moves through tunnel and snowshed on
slope of Mt. Stephen. F. L. JAQUES.

EASTBOUND . .

Fifteen cars tax 2-10-4 and helper between Spiral Tunnels in the rugged Rockies. FRED C. STOES.

THUNDER . . . The ageless mountains echo the exhausts of three Mikados as the 2-8-2's

lift Second 4 upgrade near Hector, B. C. F. L. JAQUES.

MEET . . . Eastbound Dominion holds main at Ottertail, B. C., as westbound mate enters siding behind 5925 and 5902. ERIC A. GRUBB.

DUSK . . . Helper 5803, a 2-10-2, idles downgrade. FRED C. STOES.

STUDY IN WHITE . . . West of Banff in the Sawback Range, Selkirk 5927

unrolls a plume of white over 13 cars. CANADIAN PACIFIC.

S-CURVE . . . In Kicking Horse Pass a 2-10-0 built in 1918 and a 1929 2-10-4 heel to the curvature. CANADIAN PACIFIC.

QUITE PERSONAL

THE immensity and intrigue of railroading north of the 49th parallel were first impressed upon me in the pages of a letter received from my older brother, who won his R.C.A.F. wings in 1941. He wrote of the endless frozen miles of the Maritimes and of the 4-8-4's that rolled his troop train to where a convoy rode at anchor in Halifax, N.S. Later, I saw the Rockies and Selkirks from the cab of a 2-10-4; and during the 1950's I was one of many who roamed Ontario, Quebec, New Brunswick, and Nova Scotia in search of steam. And because train-watching can be happily subjective, I developed prejudices in favor of this and that — an engine here, a train there, this station, and that bridge. I set aside a few "prejudice pictures" while selecting the illustration for this book in the thought that they might interest you too.

REGAL . . . I can't believe the British Government permitted Canadian Pacific to dub 4-6-4's 2820-2864 Royal Hudsons and to place embossed crowns on their skirts simply because the 2850 hauled Their Majesties 3100 miles without change on their 1939 tour of Canada. Someone of authority must also have examined the Hl's (in subclasses c, d, and e) and adjudged their design equal to the honor.

A. JORGENSEN.

GUTTY . . . No other word is quite so apt for the front end of Canadian National's original 4-8-4's of 1927. The overbearing, indeed, fearsome, Elesco feedwater heater, the jutting number indicator, centered headlight, outboard engine-truck journals—the cumulative effect was one of brute force. I can recall my wonderment in this roundhouse when confronted with the stored-serviceable 6105. And, I thought, how well she and the diminutive 4-6-0 in the background symbolize the CN's heritage and spirit. Truly, this photo qualifies for the "old and new." I say "new" concerning the 6105 because to me she and her sisters never aged. In a quarter-century of service they never gave an inch in esthetics to later Northerns. PHILIP R. HASTINGS.

AUTHENTIC . . . The reciprocating steam locomotive was really an astounding animal—a horizontal firetube boiler with a raging furnace at one end and a pair of huge cylinders at the other, with slabs of steel rods transmitting power in rotary fashion to spoked driving wheels as tall as a man. And the wonder is that a pair of enginemen, hanging on for dear life in a metal box called a cab fastened on the blind end of the boiler, managed to fire and direct this monster down two rails, apparently oblivious to the fact that just a thumbnail of flange prevented the whole bouncing, crashing, blasting mechanism from plunging down the nearest embankment. This fireman's-eye view of Canadian Pacific 2-8-2 5137 at work conveys a measure of the miracle; just add a shower of cinders, the heat of hades, and deafening noise to complete the great experience. DAVID PLOWDEN.

MY CHOICE . . . Canadian Pacific possessed many steam
locomotives of classic lineage but my choice of the handsomest
is its only 4-8-4's, Angus-built (1928) Kla's 3100 and 3101. See
one of them here in full stride! JIM SHAUGHNESSY.

TREASURE . . . The all-purpose American civilized the continent as surely as the plow and the rifle, only to vanish as trains and timetables outgrew the capacity of her small boiler and four-coupled axles. A rarity by World War I, the 4-4-0 was extinct a generation later. . . . Then the rumor went the rounds that the world's greatest travel system still secreted a trio of Americans in New Brunswick in deference to the light steel on a remote branch. The faithful went a-journeying in search of this Holy Grail of steam—and one chilly fall evening I stepped into the frame enginehouse at Chipman, N. B., and saw therein what you see here: Ale No. 29, constructed in 1887. Moments to remember. I was one with Galahad. PHILIP R. HASTINGS.

ONCE . . . Once upon a time, long ago in 1953, there was a CP subsidiary known as the Dominion Atlantic (or the "Land of Evangeline" Route), and its maroon passenger trains—led by elderly Pacifics and trailed by open-platform buffet-observation cars—met the steamer from St. John at dockside in Digby, N. S. This train carried one gradually away from the coast—keeping her skirts clear of the fabled Bay of Fundy tides on substantial bridges—and into the apple orchards of the Annapolis Valley. One dined on haddock and chips in the buffet, as the smoke of the G2 ahead fell over the flat-roofed express cars of Continental flair, then trailed off into the woods. The rails are there yet, but the schedule footnote in the Official Guide says: "Dayliner Air-Conditioned Rail Diesel Car; checked baggage not handled; no meals or news service." And it isn't the same. PHILIP R. HASTINGS.

THIS IS CANADA . . . From across the frozen white spaces of Saskatchewan there comes a pencil of maroon as Canadian Pacific train No. 328 bears down upon a frame interlocking plant on the last lap into Regina. KEN LIDDELL.

A. C. KALMBACH.

The steam locomotive has a working life of from 30 to 40 years. . . . The longevity of the active period of a locomotive contrasts remarkably with the comparatively brief life of some other forms of motive power. — J. R. Macken, 1946.

Kalmbach Publishing Co.

book editor — DAVID P. MORGAN
continuity — ROSEMARY ENTRINGER
design — DAVID A. STRASSMAN
layout — THEODORE E. ROSE

printing and binding — GEORGE BANTA CO., INC.

DECEMBER . . . A plume of white across the snow-smeared prairie tells of the passage of CP's Stewart Valley mixed in Saskatchewan. ROBERT HALE.